.CLASSICS.
Illustrated®

Alexandre Dumas
THE MAN IN THE IRON MASK

essay by
Beth Nachison, Ph.D.
Connecticut State University

ACCLAIM BOOKS
STUDY GUIDE

The Man in the Iron Mask

adaption by John O'Rourke
art by Ken Battlefield
cover by Jay Geldof

For Classics Illustrated Study Guides
computer recoloring by Colorgraphix
editor: Madeleine Robins
assistant editor: Gregg Sanderson
design: Scott Friedlander

Classics Illustrated: The Man in the Iron Mask © Twin Circle Publishing Co.
a division of Frawley Enterprises; licensed to First Classics, Inc.
All new material and compilation © 1997 by Acclaim Books, Inc.

Dale-Chall R.L.: 8.2

ISBN 1-57840-037-6

Classics Illustrated® is a registered trademark of the Frawley Corporation.

Acclaim Books, New York, NY
Printed in the United States

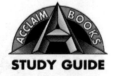

STUDY GUIDE

THE MAN IN THE IRON MASK

Alexandre Dumas

ONE NIGHT IN THE YEAR 1661, THE STEPS OF THREE MEN RESOUNDED IN THE COURTYARD OF THE BASTILLE. THE TURNKEY, WHO LED THE WAY, HELD HIS HEAD DOWN. HE SEEMED AFRAID TO KEEP HIS EARS OPEN. IN THESE TOWERS SECRETS WERE BURIED AS WELL AS MEN-- SECRETS OF THE MIGHTY, SECRETS SO TERRIBLE THAT EVEN TO KNOW OF THEIR EXISTENCE COULD COST A MAN HIS LIFE.

ARAMIS, FORMER MUSKETEER AND NOW BISHOP OF VANNES, HAD COME TO CONFESS A MYSTERIOUS PRISONER KNOWN ONLY AS MARCHIALI. BAISEMEAUX, GOVERNOR OF THE BASTILLE, ACCOMPANIED ARAMIS TO THE CELL.

WHEN THEY REACHED THE DOOR. . .

THE RULES DO NOT ALLOW THE GOVERNOR TO HEAR THE PRISONER'S CONFESSION.

A MOMENT LATER, ARAMIS WAS ALONE WITH THE PRISONER OF THE BASTILLE.

EVERY PRISONER HAS COMMITTED SOME CRIME. WHAT CRIME, THEN, HAVE YOU COMMITTED?

AS MY CONSCIENCE DOES NOT ACCUSE ME, I AVER I AM NOT A CRIMINAL.

WE ARE OFTEN CRIMINALS IN THE EYES OF THE GREAT, MERELY FOR KNOWING THAT A CRIME HAS BEEN COMMITTED.

YOU ARE HERE TO REVEAL IMPORTANT MATTERS TO ME. WHO ARE YOU?

DO YOU REMEMBER ONCE, IN THE VILLAGE WHERE YOU SPENT YOUR YOUTH, SEEING A CAVALIER, ACCOMPANIED BY A LADY IN BLACK?

I DO. AND I RECOGNIZED YOU AS THAT CAVALIER.

THEN KNOW THIS ALSO. IF THE KING WERE TO LEARN THIS EVENING OF MY PRESENCE HERE, I WOULD TOMORROW SEE THE GLITTER OF THE EXECUTIONER'S AX. NOW, WHAT MORE DO YOU REMEMBER?

I REMEMBER WELL A WOMAN WHO CAME TO SEE ME EVERY MONTH. SHE, MY TUTOR, AND MY NURSE WERE THE ONLY PERSONS I EVER SPOKE TO.

"A HOUSE WHICH I NEVER QUITTED, A GARDEN SURROUNDED WITH WALLS I COULD NOT CLEAR, THESE CONSTITUTED MY RESIDENCE WHEN I WAS A BOY.

"I LIVED AS CHILDREN DO, AS BIRDS, AS PLANTS AND THE SUN DO. THEN, ONE DAY, WHEN I HAD JUST TURNED MY FIFTEENTH YEAR . . .

"IT WAS VERY HOT AND I HAD FALLEN ASLEEP. I AWOKE TO HEAR MY TUTOR AND NURSE TALKING EXCITEDLY.

THE LETTER! THE LAST LETTER FROM THE QUEEN! IT'S IN THE WELL! THE WIND BLEW IT FROM MY HAND!

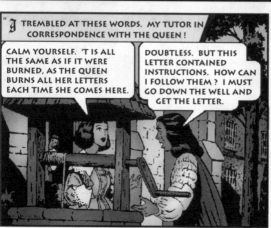

"I TREMBLED AT THESE WORDS. MY TUTOR IN CORRESPONDENCE WITH THE QUEEN!

CALM YOURSELF. 'TIS ALL THE SAME AS IF IT WERE BURNED, AS THE QUEEN BURNS ALL HER LETTERS EACH TIME SHE COMES HERE.

DOUBTLESS. BUT THIS LETTER CONTAINED INSTRUCTIONS. HOW CAN I FOLLOW THEM? I MUST GO DOWN THE WELL AND GET THE LETTER.

THEN THE LADY WHO COMES TO SEE ME EVERY MONTH IS THE QUEEN!

COME, WE WILL GET A LADDER LONG ENOUGH TO REACH THE WATER.

"WHEN THEY LEFT, I SPRANG THROUGH THE WINDOW AND RAN TO THE WELL.

"SOMETHING WHITE AND LUMINOUS GLISTENED IN THE GREEN RIPPLES.

" I LOWERED THE CORD AND BUCKET TO WITHIN THREE FEET OF THE WATER. THEN I SLID INTO THE ABYSS.

" I WAS SEIZED WITH GIDDINESS AND THE HAIR ROSE ON MY HEAD. BUT AT LAST I GAINED THE WATER AND SEIZED THE LETTER.

" I CONCEALED IT IN MY SHIRT AND REGAINED THE BRINK.

"THEN I RUSHED INTO THE SHRUBBERY TO READ MY PRIZE.

" **I** READ ENOUGH TO LEARN THAT I MUST BE HIGH-BORN, SINCE THE QUEEN EARNESTLY COMMENDED ME TO THE CARE OF MY TUTOR. I HAD JUST TIME TO CONCEAL THE LETTER WHEN I WAS DISCOVERED. "

PHILIPPE! YOU ARE WET THROUGH! WHAT HAS HAPPENED TO YOU?

" **T**HAT NIGHT, I WAS SIEZED WITH A VIOLENT CHILL AND AN ATTACK OF DELIRIUM, DURING WHICH I RELATED THE WHOLE ADVENTURE. "

THE QUEEN... THE QUEEN... COMES TO SEE ME....

LOOK! UNDER HIS PILLOW! THE QUEEN S LETTER!

POOR LAD, WHAT WILL HAPPEN TO HIM NOW?

DOUBTLESS, MY TUTOR, NOT DARING TO KEEP THE MATTER SECRET, WROTE ALL TO THE QUEEN, FOR SOON AFTER, I WAS BROUGHT HERE TO THE BASTILLE.

NOW I AM WEARY OF SPEAKING. IT IS YOUR TURN. CAN YOU TELL ME WHAT HAPPENED TO MY NURSE AND TUTOR?

THEY WERE MADE TO DISAPPEAR BY THE SUREST WAY POSSIBLE. BY POISON.

MY ENEMY MUST INDEED BE CRUEL TO MURDER THOSE INNOCENT PEOPLE.

IN YOUR FAMILY, MONSEIGNEUR, NECESSITY IS STERN. BUT ONE MORE QUESTION. IN YOUR HOUSE, WERE THERE EITHER LOOKING GLASSES OR MIRRORS?

WHAT IS THE MEANING OF THOSE TWO WORDS? I HAVE NO KNOWLEDGE OF THEM.

THEY ARE OBJECTS WHICH REFLECT ONE'S OWN IMAGE. TELL ME FURTHER, WERE YOU INSTRUCTED IN HISTORY?

VERY LITTLE.

IT WAS DONE BY DESIGN. JUST AS THEY DEPRIVED YOU OF MIRRORS, WHICH REFLECT THE PRESENT, SO THEY LEFT YOU IN IGNORANCE OF HISTORY, WHICH REFLECTS THE PAST.

LISTEN, THEN. I WILL TELL YOU WHAT HAS PASSED IN FRANCE FROM THE TIME OF YOUR BIRTH.

" ON THE FIFTH OF SEPTEMBER, 1638, ANNE OF AUSTRIA, WIFE OF LOUIS XIII, GAVE BIRTH TO A SON.

" BUT WHILE THE COURT AND KING WERE REJOICING OVER THE EVENT, THE QUEEN, ALONE IN HER ROOM EXCEPT FOR A MIDWIFE, GAVE BIRTH TO A SECOND SON.

" THE MIDWIFE, WHO LATER BECAME YOUR NURSE, RAN AT ONCE AND WHISPERED THE NEWS TO THE KING.

" THE KING'S JOY CHANGED TO TERROR.

TWIN SONS WILL MEAN DISCORD AND CIVIL WAR.

" THE KING CONSULTED WITH HIS PRIME MINISTER.

TWIN SONS WILL SURELY BRING ABOUT A WAR OF SUCCESSION. THE SECOND SON MUST BE TAKEN AWAY WHERE NONE SHALL KNOW OF HIS EXISTENCE.

IT SHALL BE DONE. MY DYNASTY MUST BE PRESERVED.

" AND SO, ONE NIGHT SOON AFTER, THE SECOND SON WAS SPIRITED AWAY FROM THE PALACE. "

SO COMPLETELY DID THAT SECOND SON DISAPPEAR THAT NOT A SOUL IN FRANCE, SAVE HIS MOTHER, IS AWARE OF HIS EXISTENCE.

HIS MOTHER... HIS MOTHER, WHO HAS CAST HIM OFF.

HAVE YOU A PORTRAIT OF THE KING, LOUIS XIV, WHO AT THIS MOMENT REIGNS UPON THE THRONE?

HERE.

AND NOW, HERE IS A MIRROR.

A CRIME WAS COMMITTED AGAINST YOU IN RENDERING THOSE DIFFERENT IN FORTUNE WHO NATURE CREATED THE SAME IN THE WOMB. THE PUNISHMENT SHOULD RESTORE THE BALANCE.

BY WHICH YOU MEAN. . .

THAT WHEN I PUT YOU ON YOUR BROTHER'S THRONE, HE SHALL TAKE YOUR PLACE IN PRISON.

NOW, ADIEU, MONSEIGNEUR, UNTIL I COME TO FETCH YOU FROM THESE GLOOMY WALLS.

A MOMENT LATER, ARAMIS LEFT THE CELL AND REJOINED THE GOVERNOR OF THE BASTILLE.

WHAT A LONG CONFESSION ! WHO WOULD BELIEVE THAT A RECLUSE HAD SINS SO LONG TO TELL OF !

A FEW DAYS LATER, ARAMIS CALLED ON MONSIEUR FOUQUET, FRANCE'S SUPERINTENDENT OF FINANCES.

AH, MY FRIEND, IS ALL IN READINESS FOR THE FESTIVAL YOU ARE TO GIVE IN HONOR OF THE KING? EVERYONE TALKS OF HOW SPLENDID IT IS TO BE.

THE FESTIVAL IS APPROACHING. MONEY IS DEPARTING.

HAVE I NOT TOLD YOU THAT MONEY IS MY WORRY?

YES, YOU PROMISED ME MILLIONS.

YOU SHALL HAVE THEM-- THE DAY AFTER THE KING COMES TO YOUR CHATEAU AT VAUX FOR THE FESTIVAL.

AND NOW I WOULD LIKE A LETTER FROM YOU. I WISH TO HAVE A LETTRE DE CACHET.

LETTRE DE CACHET! DO YOU WISH TO PUT SOMEBODY IN THE BASTILLE?

ON THE CONTRARY, I WISH TO LET SOMEONE OUT.

WHO?

A POOR LAD NAMED SELDON, WHO HAS BEEN BASTILLED THESE TEN YEARS FOR TWO LATIN VERSES HE WROTE.

WHAT! YOU KNEW OF THIS INJUSTICE AND YOU NEVER TOLD ME?

'TWAS ONLY YESTERDAY HIS MOTHER APPLIED TO ME. POOR WOMAN, SHE LIVES IN DEEPEST POVERTY.

FOUQUET QUICKLY WROTE THE LETTER. THEN HE TOOK 10,000 FRANCS FROM HIS DESK.

SET THE SON AT LIBERTY AND GIVE THIS TO THE MOTHER. BUT DO NOT TELL HER THAT . . .

THAT WHAT, MONSEIGNEUR?

THAT SHE IS NOW 10,000 FRANCS RICHER THAN I. SHE WOULD SAY I AM INDEED A POOR SUPERINTENDENT OF FINANCES.

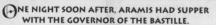

ONE NIGHT SOON AFTER, ARAMIS HAD SUPPER WITH THE GOVERNOR OF THE BASTILLE.

TO SEE YOU BOOTED AS A CAVALIER REMINDS ME OF PAST DAYS.

IT SHOULD. YOU WERE A MUSKETEER WITH US-- WITH ATHOS AND PORTHOS AND D'ARTAGNAN. MORE WINE, BAISEMEAUX. LET US CELEBRATE THE OLD DAYS.

AN HOUR LATER, A CLATTER WAS HEARD IN THE COURTYARD. A COURIER HAD ARRIVED WITH A MESSAGE FOR THE GOVERNOR.

LET HIM GO TO THE DEVIL. I AM AT SUPPER.

TAKE CARE, FRIEND. THE MESSAGE MAY BE IMPORTANT.

BAISEMEAUX HAD THE MESSAGE BROUGHT UP.

AN ORDER OF RELEASE! THEY SEIZE A MAN, KEEP HIM FOR YEARS, THEN, WITHOUT WARNING, SAY, "RELEASE HIM AT ONCE." BAH! LET HIM WAIT UNTIL MORNING.

BOOTED THOUGH I BE, I AM A PRIEST. I ENTREAT YOU TO ABRIDGE THIS POOR MAN'S SUFFERING AT ONCE. GOD WILL REPAY YOU IN PARADISE.

IN THE MIDDLE OF OUR SUPPER? OH, VERY WELL, THEN, IF YOU WISH IT.

AS THE GOVERNOR CALLED FOR HIS MEN, ARAMIS CHANGED THE ORDER FOR ANOTHER.

THEN . . .

I WILL HAVE THE MAJOR GO AND OPEN THE CELL OF MONSIEUR SELDON.

YOU MEAN TO SAY MARCHIALI.

MARCHIALI? NO, NO-- SELDON!

I SAW SELDON IN LETTERS LARGE AS THAT.

AND I READ MARCHIALI IN CHARACTERS AS LARGE AS THIS.

LOOK.

YES, 'TIS PLAINLY WRITTEN --MARCHIALI. THE MAN I HAVE ORDERS TO WATCH MOST CAREFULLY. I DO NOT UNDERSTAND IT.

BAISEMEAUX BECAME VERY SUSPICIOUS.

MARCHIALI IS THE VERY PRISONER WHOM A CERTAIN PRIEST OF THE JESUITS CAME TO VISIT THE OTHER NIGHT IN SO SECRET A MANNER.

WITH US, MONSIEUR, FOR YOU, TOO , ARE A MEMBER OF THE ORDER, IT IS GOOD THAT THE MAN OF TODAY FORGET THE MAN OF YESTERDAY.

IF A SUPERIOR OFFICER OF THE JESUITS GIVES YOU ORDERS, YOU WILL OBEY ?

NEVER DOUBT IT, MONSEIGNEUR.

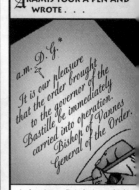
ARAMIS TOOK A PEN AND WROTE . . .

a.m.D.G.*

It is our pleasure that the order brought to the governor of the Bastille be immediately carried into operation.

Bishop of Vannes
General of the Order.

*ad majorem Dei gloriam, which means, "to the greater glory of God".

BAISEMEAUX WAS ASTONISHED.

YOU ARE GENERAL OF THE ORDER ! TO THINK THAT I HAVE DARED TO TREAT YOU AS AN EQUAL !

SAY NOTHING OF IT, OLD COMRADE. TO YOU I GIVE MY PROTECTION AND FRIENDSHIP. TO ME YOU GIVE YOUR OBEDIENCE.

HAVE YOUR MEN BRING THE PRISONER MARCHIALI HERE.

A SHORT TIME LATER, THE DUNGEON RENDERED UP ITS PREY.

YOU WILL SWEAR NEVER TO REVEAL ANYTHING YOU HAVE SEEN OR HEARD IN THE BASTILLE.

PHILIPPE KISSED A CRUCIFIX, IN TOKEN OF HIS WORD.

NOW THAT YOU ARE FREE, WHITHER DO YOU INTEND GOING ?

THEN ARAMIS STEPPED OUT OF THE SHADOWS.

I AM HERE TO RENDER THE GENTLEMAN WHATEVER SERVICE HE MAY ASK.

SOON PHILIPPE AND ARAMIS ENTERED A CARRIAGE WHICH HAD BEEN KEPT IN READINESS. A FEW MINUTES LATER-- NO MORE WALLS ON EITHER SIDE; LIBERTY EVERYWHERE, HEAVEN EVERYWHERE.

THERE IS YET ANOTHER OBSTACLE -- MY CONSCIENCE.

IT IS USELESS TO FLASH BRIGHT VISIONS BEFORE THE EYES OF ONE WHO LOVES DARKNESS. DO YOU WISH A MORE HUMBLE LIFE?

I KNOW OF A PLACE OF WHICH NO ONE IN FRANCE SUSPECTS THE EXISTENCE. THE SUN THERE IS SOFT, THE SOIL RICH, THE GAME PLENTIFUL.

YOU CAN GO THERE AND LIVE IN SAFETY, PEACE AND COMFORT. OR YOU CAN TAKE THE THRONE AND RISK DEATH. WHICH WILL YOU ACCEPT?

BEFORE I ANSWER, LET ME WALK ON THE GROUND AND CONSULT THAT STILL VOICE WITHIN ME WHICH HEAVEN SENDS US ALL.

WHEN PHILIPPE RETURNED TO THE CARRIAGE...

LET US GO WHERE THE CROWN OF FRANCE IS TO BE FOUND!

PROVIDENCE HAS SPOKEN. NOW LET US RESUME OUR CONVERSATION. HAVE YOU READ THE NOTES I HAD SMUGGLED TO YOU TO AQUAINT YOU WITH YOUR COURT?

I KNOW THEM BY HEART.

"MY MOTHER, ANNE OF AUSTRIA, ALL HER SORROWS, HER PAINFUL MALADY. OH, I KNOW HER.

"COLBERT, MY MINISTER, IS UGLY AND DARK-BROWED. HE IS THE MORTAL ENEMY OF MONSIEUR FOUQUET.

"D'ARTAGNAN IS THE CAPTAIN OF MY MUSKETEERS. TO THIS BRAVE MAN THE CROWN OF FRANCE OWES SO MUCH IT OWES EVERYTHING. AND PORTHOS, THE HERCULES OF FRANCE. I SEE HIM, TOO, IN MY MIND'S EYE.

D'ARTAGNAN AND PORTHOS. YOUR FRIENDS, MONSIEUR.

YES, I CAN WELL SAY, "MY FRIENDS."

WHAT OF MONSIEUR FOUQUET? WHAT DO YOU WISH ME TO DO FOR HIM?

WHEN YOU SHALL HAVE PAID HIS DEBTS AND RESTORED THE COUNTRY'S FINANCES TO A SOUND CONDITION, WE SHALL RETIRE HIM TO HIS PLEASURES.

AND FOR YOURSELF?

FIRST, I WILL BE MADE A CARDINAL AND PRIME MINISTER OF FRANCE. THEN, SINCE I SHALL HAVE GIVEN YOU THE THRONE OF FRANCE, YOU WILL CONFER ON ME THE THRONE OF ST. PETER.

I WILL DO ALL THAT YOU DIRECT.

PHILIPPE AND ARAMIS RESUMED THEIR PLACES IN THE CARRIAGE. THEY SPED TOWARD VAUX, WHERE KING LOUIS XIV WOULD COME TO ATTEND FOUQUET'S FESTIVAL IN HIS HONOR.

THE NEXT DAY, AT VAUX, ARAMIS AND FOUQUET AWAITED THE ARRIVAL OF LOUIS XIV.

THE KING WILL SOON BE HERE. YOU CAN SEE HIS PROCESSION IN THE DISTANCE.

HE CARES FOR ME BUT LITTLE. BUT AS MY GUEST, HE IS MORE SACRED THAN EVER TO ME.

ARE YOU COMFORTABLE, MY FRIEND ? WHAT APARTMENT HAVE YOU CHOSEN FOR YOUR LODGINGS ?

THE BLUE ROOM ON THE SECOND STORY.

THE ROOM DIRECTLY OVER THE KING'S ? WHAT AN IDEA, TO CONDEMN YOURSELF TO A ROOM WHERE YOU CANNOT STIR FOR FEAR OF DISTURBING HIS MAJESTY.

DO NOT FEAR. DURING THE NIGHT, I SLEEP OR READ IN MY BED.

AND YOUR SERVANTS ?

I HAVE ONLY ONE PERSON WITH ME. ADIEU, MONSEIGNEUR. I SHALL SEE YOU LATER.

*T*HAT NIGHT, A SPLENDID BANQUET WAS HELD FOR THE ROYAL GUESTS.

I AM HUMILIATED ! FOUQUET HAS TREASURES UNKNOWN TO MY PALACE.

*A*FTER THE FEAST, THE KING WENT TO HIS ROOM.

TELL MONSIEUR COLBERT I WISH TO SEE HIM.

*M*EANWHILE, IN THE ROOM ABOVE, ARAMIS HAD A VISITOR.

WELCOME, D'ARTAGNAN ! PORTHOS WOULD WELCOME YOU, TOO. BUT HE HAS DINED WELL AND YOU REMEMBER HOW SOUNDLY HE SLEEPS.

ARAMIS, DO YOU REMEMBER HOW YOU USED TO HAVE FAITH IN MY INSTINCTIVE FEELINGS ? WELL, AN INSTINCT TELLS ME YOU ARE PLOTTING SOMETHING.

WHAT NONSENSE !

NO-- A VOICE WHICH HAS NEVER YET DECEIVED ME SPEAKS WITHIN ME. IT IS THE KING YOU ARE CONSPIRING AGAINST.

YOU ARE MAD. BESIDES, DO YOU NOT HAVE YOUR GUARDS AND MUSKETEERS HERE TO PROTECT HIM?

TRUE. BUT GRANT ME, ARAMIS, THE WORD OF A TRUE FRIEND. SAY THERE IS NO PLOT.

IF I THINK OF HARMING THE SON OF ANNE OF AUSTRIA, THE TRUE KING OF THIS REALM, MAY HEAVEN'S LIGHTNING BLAST ME WHERE I STAND!

VERY WELL. I BELIEVE YOU.

THEN D'ARTAGNAN WOKE PORTHOS.

COME, I WILL TAKE YOU TO YOUR ROOM.

GOOD NIGHT, MY FRIENDS. IN TEN MINUTES, I SHALL BE FAST ASLEEP.

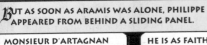 BUT AS SOON AS ARAMIS WAS ALONE, PHILIPPE APPEARED FROM BEHIND A SLIDING PANEL.

MONSIEUR D'ARTAGNAN IS EXTREMELY SUSPICIOUS. HE SEEMS VERY DEVOTED TO THE KING.

HE IS AS FAITHFUL AS A DOG. BUT HE BITES SOMETIMES.

WHAT ARE WE TO DO NOW?

YOU WILL OBSERVE THE CEREMONY OF THE KING'S RETIRING, SO AS TO LEARN HOW IT IS PERFORMED.

HE PUSHED ASIDE A PORTION OF THE FLOORING.

CAN YOU SEE?

YES. MONSIEUR COLBERT IS WITH THE KING.

WHAT! IT BODES ILL FOR MONSIEUR FOUQUET. LET ME SEE.

COLBERT, FOUQUET HAS ECLIPSED ME. HIS TABLE GROANS WITH DELIGHTS THAT HAVE NEVER GRACED MY OWN. WHERE DOES HE GET HIS WEALTH?

FIVE MINUTES LATER, D'ARTAGNAN STOOD BEFORE LOUIS XIV.

PLACE MONSIEUR FOUQUET UNDER ARREST!

WHAT? ARREST HIM IN HIS OWN HOUSE? WHILE YOU ARE UNDER HIS ROOF-- HIS GUEST?

THE KING IS MASTER, WHEREVER HE MAY BE.

THE KING IS MASTER IN A MAN'S HOUSE ONLY WHEN HE HAS DRIVEN THE OWNER OUT OF IT. THINK, SIRE, DO NOT BRING SHAME UPON YOUR HEAD.

I HATE HIM! TOMORROW HE SHALL FALL SO LOW THAT EVERYONE WILL KNOW I AM INDEED GREATER THAN HE. GO! KEEP HIM UNDER YOUR GUARD!

IT IS YOUR WISH, AND IT SHALL BE DONE. BUT, SIRE! TO ARREST IN HIS OWN HOUSE A MAN WHO IS RUINING HIMSELF TO PLEASE YOU!

GUARD MONSIEUR FOUQUET TONIGHT AND RETURN IN THE MORNING FOR FURTHER ORDERS. NOW LEAVE ME!

WHEN D'ARTAGNAN HAD GONE, THE KING THREW HIMSELF ON HIS BED.

WHILE ABOVE HIS HEAD...

NOW THE KING WILL SLEEP. HAVING RETIRED AS A CROWNED SOVEREIGN, HE WILL AWAKEN IN CAPTIVITY.

MY BROTHER WILL DISAPPEAR SO SIMPLY?

A SECRET CONTRIVANCE WHICH YIELDS TO THE PRESSURE OF A FINGER WILL LOWER THE BED TO AN UNDERGROUND PASSAGEWAY. IT WILL RETURN EMPTY.

THEN THE SAME CONTRIVANCE WILL LOWER A PORTION OF THIS FLOOR, AND YOU WILL BE IN THE KING'S PLACE. FROM THAT MOMENT, YOU ALONE WILL RULE.

I GO NOW TO ALERT MY FAITHFUL PORTHOS, WHO WILL HELP ME RECEIVE THE DEPOSED KING.

BELOW, EXHAUSTED BY HIS FURY, THE KING BEGAN TO FALL ASLEEP. AS HIS EYES CLOSED, HE FANCIED A FACE GAZING DOWN AT HIM IN PROFOUND PITY--A FACE AS MUCH HIS OWN AS THOUGH IT WERE REFLECTED IN A MIRROR.

A GENTLE, EASY MOVEMENT, AS REGULAR AS THAT BY WHICH A VESSEL PLUNGES BENEATH THE WAVES, SUCCEEDED TO THE IMMOBILITY OF THE BED.

THE CEILING SEEMED TO BE GRADUALLY GETTING FURTHER AND FURTHER AWAY.

THE KING, HALF-AWAKENED, THOUGHT HIMSELF UNDER THE INFLUENCE OF A TERRIBLE DREAM. SOMETHING COLD AND GLOOMY SEEMED TO INFECT THE AIR.

AFTER A MINUTE WHICH SEEMED AN AGE TO THE KING, THE BED REACHED A LEVEL OF AIR BLACK AND STILL AS DEATH. THEN IT STOPPED.

IT IS TIME TO WAKEN FROM THIS MAD DREAM. COME, LET ME WAKE UP.

THEN . . .

WHAT IS THE MEANING OF THIS JEST?

IT IS NO JEST. WE ARE YOUR MASTERS, NOW. BE GOOD ENOUGH TO FOLLOW US.

WHAT DO YOU INTEND TO DO WITH THE KING OF FRANCE?

YOU DESERVE TO BE BROKEN ON THE WHEEL FOR CALLING YOURSELF THAT.

THE KING WAS LED TO A CARRIAGE THAT WAITED AT THE END OF THE PASSAGEWAY.

IT SEEMS I HAVE FALLEN INTO THE HANDS OF ASSASSINS.

THE CARRIAGE DROVE TO THE BASTILLE, WHERE ARAMIS ROUSED THE GOVERNOR.

WHAT IS THE MATTER NOW? WHOM HAVE YOU BROUGHT ME?

LET US GO TO YOUR ROOM. I WILL EXPLAIN THERE.

A FEW MOMENTS LATER . . .

IT APPEARS YOU WERE QUITE RIGHT THE OTHER DAY ABOUT THE ORDER OF RELEASE. IT WAS FOR SELDON, NOT MARCHIALI.

I AM A LOST MAN!

FAR FROM IT. SINCE I HAVE MARCHIALI BACK, IT IS JUST THE SAME AS IF HE NEVER LEFT.

BUT WHY DID YOU BRING HIM BACK?

FROM YOU, MY FRIEND, I HAVE NO SECRETS. YOU HAVE NO DOUBT NOTED THE RESEMBLANCE BETWEEN THAT FELLOW AND THE KING?

YES.

WELL, THE WRETCH MADE USE OF HIS LIBERTY BY PRETENDING TO BE THE KING HIMSELF! THE KING IS FURIOUS!

LET US RETURN THIS MADMAN TO HIS CELL AT ONCE!

THEY RETURNED TO THE COURTYARD.

AH! SO YOU ARE BACK, YOU MISERABLE WRETCH.

A MOMENT LATER, THE KING, TOO STUNNED TO SPEAK, WAS LED TO PHILIPPE'S CELL.

IN WITH YOU!

SOON ARAMIS AND PORTHOS WERE BACK AT THEIR CARRIAGE.

BACK TO VAUX, AS FAST AS POSSIBLE!

A MAN IS LIGHT AND EASY WHEN HE HAS FAITHFULLY SERVED HIS TRUE KING. THE HORSES WILL MOVE AS FAST AS THOUGH THEY HAD NOTHING AT ALL BEHIND THEM.

THE KING, ALONE IN HIS CELL. WAS STILL IN A STUPOR.

AM I DEAD? IS THIS WHAT IS TERMED HELL?

THEN HE LOOKED DOWN.

A CRY ESCAPED HIM, AND HE RETURNED TO HIS SENSES.

A PRISONER! I--I, A PRISONER!

THERE IS A GOVERNOR IN THIS PLACE. I WILL SUMMON HIM TO ME.

WHERE IS THE GOVERNOR? I WANT TO SPEAK TO THE GOVERNOR!

BUT NO VOICE REPLIED TO HIS.

He broke a chair and used the leg to strike the door.

OPEN! OPEN IN THE KING'S NAME!

When no one answered, he leaped from the table to the window and broke a pane of glass.

THE GOVERNOR! I WANT TO SEE THE GOVERNOR!

In time, a jailer came to bring him food.

YOU HAVE BROKEN YOUR CHAIR. WHY, YOU MUST HAVE GONE QUITE MAD.

MONSIEUR, ASK THE GOVERNOR TO COME TO ME.

COME, MY BOY. YOU HAVE BROKEN YOUR CHAIR AND MADE A GREAT DISTURBANCE. PROMISE ME NOT TO BEGIN OVER AGAIN, AND I WILL NOT SAY A WORD TO THE GOVERNOR.

I WISH TO SEE THE GOVERNOR!

AH, YOUR EYES ARE BECOMING WILD. I SHALL HAVE TO TAKE AWAY YOUR KNIFE.

THE JAILER LEFT. NOW THE KING'S RAGE AND FRENZY KNEW NO BOUNDS.

HE TORE AT THE DOOR WITH HIS NAILS AND UTTERED WILD AND FEARFUL CRIES.

TWO HOURS AFTERWARD, LOUIS XIV COULD NOT BE RECOGNIZED AS A KING-- A GENTLEMAN-- A HUMAN BEING.

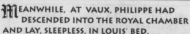

MEANWHILE, AT VAUX, PHILIPPE HAD DESCENDED INTO THE ROYAL CHAMBER AND LAY, SLEEPLESS, IN LOUIS' BED.

I AM NOW FACE TO FACE WITH MY DESTINY.

TOWARD MORNING, A SHADOW GLIDED INTO THE ROOM.

WELL, MONSIEUR?

ALL IS DONE, SIRE.

HE IS IN YOUR CELL. THE GOVERNOR OF THE BASTILLE SUSPECTS NOTHING.

AT THAT MOMENT, DAWN CAME. A MINUTE LATER, THERE WAS A KNOCK ON THE DOOR.

THAT MUST BE D'ARTAGNAN TO REQUEST FURTHER ORDERS ON THE DISPOSITION OF MONSIEUR FOUQUET. NOW WE BEGIN THE ATTACK.

TO START WITH D'ARTAGNAN WOULD BE MADNESS. THE KEENEST SCENT IN FRANCE WOULD BE SURE TO DETECT SOMETHING HAS TAKEN PLACE IN THIS ROOM. I WILL SEND HIM AWAY.

D'ARTAGNAN WAS ASTOUNDED WHEN THE DOOR OPENED.

ARAMIS! YOU HERE?

THE KING DOES NOT WISH TO BE DISTURBED. HOWEVER, HE INSTRUCTS YOU TO SET MONSIEUR FOUQUET AT LIBERTY. I SHALL GO WITH YOU TO WITNESS HIS DELIGHT.

BUT HOW HAVE YOU BECOME SO MUCH A FAVORITE OF THE KING THAT YOU CAN TRANSMIT ORDERS IN HIS NAME? YOU HAVE NEVER SPOKEN TO HIM MORE THAN TWICE IN YOUR LIFE.

THE FACT IS, I HAVE SPOKEN TO HIM MORE THAN A HUNDRED TIMES, ONLY WE HAVE KEPT IT SECRET. SO NOW YOU UNDERSTAND EVERYTHING.

AH, OF COURSE. NOW I UNDERSTAND.

NO, I DO NOT UNDERSTAND-- YET.

SO, CAPTAIN, YOU HAVE BROUGHT THE BISHOP OF VANNES TO SEE YOUR PRISONER.

AND SOMETHING BETTER STILL-- LIBERTY. YOU ARE FREE, BY HIS MAJESTY'S ORDER.

I DO NOT UNDERSTAND. WHAT DOES THIS MEAN?

THE KING BELIEVES YOU TO BE GUILTY OF STEALING PUBLIC FUNDS. HE IS ALSO ENVIOUS OF THE MAGNITUDE OF THE FESTIVAL YOU ARE GIVING IN HIS HONOR. HE PROCLAIMS YOU A TRAITOR AND A THIEF.

THEN I DO NOT SEE-- WHY AM I PARDONED?

DO YOU REALLY THINK IT LIKELY THE KING WOULD PARDON YOU?

YOU ALARM ME. YOU ARE CONCEALING SOMETHING. WHAT IS THERE BETWEEN YOU AND THE KING?

A SECRET. ONE OF A NATURE TO CHANGE THE INTERESTS OF THE KING OF FRANCE.

THEN ARAMIS TOLD FOUQUET EVERYTHING.

GREAT GOD! THE KING DETHRONED? IMPRISONED? AND SUCH A CRIME HAS BEEN COMMITTED UNDER MY ROOF?

YOU DARED DO THIS -- WHILE THE KING WAS MY GUEST -- IN THE PROTECTION OF MY HOUSE?

YOUR HOUSE, YES. FOR MONSIEUR COLBERT CANNOT HAVE THE KING ROB YOU OF IT NOW.

YOU DARED TO COMMIT THIS CRIME HERE? THIS ABOMINABLE CRIME WHICH DISHONORS MY NAME FOREVER!

CRIME? YOU ARE NOT IN YOUR SENSES, MONSEIGNEUR. THE KING'S IMPRISONMENT SAVES YOUR LIFE!

YOU MAY HAVE BEEN ACTING ON MY BEHALF, BUT I WILL NOT ACCEPT YOUR SERVICES. YOU WILL LEAVE MY HOUSE. I GIVE YOU FOUR HOURS TO PUT YOURSELF OUT OF THE KINGS REACH.

GO AT ONCE -- TO SAVE YOUR LIFE. I GO TO MY SOVEREIGN TO SAVE MY HONOR.

ARAMIS HURRIED TO PORTHOS' ROOM.

LOST! ALL IS LOST! SHALL I WARN PHILIPPE? TAKE HIM WITH ME? CIVIL WAR WOULD FOLLOW.

LET DESTINY BE FUFILLED. CONDEMNED WAS PHILIPPE, LET HIM REMAIN SO.

A FEW MINUTES LATER, D'ARTAGNAN WAS SURPRISED TO SEE ARAMIS AND PORTHOS RIDING OFF.

ADIEU, OLD FRIEND!

ON ANY OTHER OCCASION, I SHOULD SAY THOSE TWO WERE MAKING THIER ESCAPE. BUT LET ME ATTEND TO MY OWN AFFAIRS; THAT IS QUITE ENOUGH.

MEANWHILE, FOUQUET HAD RUSHED TO THE BASTILLE. WHEN HE ENTERED THE KING'S CELL . . .

HAVE YOU COME TO ASSASSINATE ME, MONSIEUR FOUQUET?

SIRE, DO YOU NOT RECOGNIZE THE MOST FAITHFUL OF YOUR FRIENDS?

A FRIEND -- YOU?

I AM THE MOST RESPECTFUL OF YOUR SERVANTS.

WAS IT NOT YOU WHO HAD ME BROUGHT HERE?

YOU CANNOT BELIEVE ME TO BE GUILTY OF SUCH AN ACT.

AND FOUQUET TOLD THE KING EVERYTHING HE KNEW.

SO! IT WAS THE BISHOP OF VANNES WHO LED THIS PLOT. AND THIS IMPOSTOR, PHILIPPE! HE MUST DIE!

ROYAL BLOOD CANNOT BE SHED ON THE SCAFFOLD.

ROYAL BLOOD! YOU BELIEVE THAT RIDICULOUS STORY OF THE DOUBLE BIRTH?

I DOUBT IT NOT, SIRE. PHILIPPE OF FRANCE IS YOUR BROTHER. THERE MUST BE NO PUBLIC TRIAL. THE AUGUST NAME OF YOUR MOTHER MUST NOT BE TOUCHED BY SCANDAL.

COME. LET US RETURN TO VAUX AND SEE THIS PHILIPPE. BUT FIRST, I SHALL STOP AT THE LOUVRE AND CHANGE MY CLOTHES.

SOON, BAISEMEAUX, COMPLETELY BEWILDERED BY THESE STRANGE EVENTS, WAS WATCHING MARCHIALI ONCE AGAIN LEAVE THE BASTILLE.

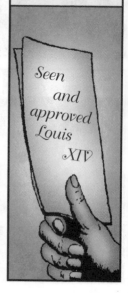

FOUQUET HAD GIVEN HIM AN ORDER TO RELEASE THE PRISONER AND ON IT THE PRISONER HIMSELF HAD WRITTEN . . .

Seen
and
approved
Louis
XIV

AT VAUX, PHILIPPE HAD BEGUN TO PLAY HIS PART, EXPECTING ARAMIS AT ANY MOMENT TO APPEAR AT HIS SIDE TO GIVE HIM COUNSEL..

WHEN PHILIPPE WAS DRESSED, SEVERAL MEMBERS OF THE COURT ENTERED. HE TREMBLED WHEN HE RECOGNIZED HIS MOTHER.

THIS IS THE WOMAN WHO SACRIFICED HER CHILD FOR REASONS OF STATE.

BUT SHE IS SO NOBLE, SO RAVAGED BY HER ILLNESSES. I WILL TRY TO LOVE HER AS A SON SHOULD.

PHILIPPE DREADED MOST THE APPEARANCE OF LOUIS' WIFE. BUT . . .

THE QUEEN DESIRES YOU TO KNOW THAT SHE IS FATIGUED AND WILL KEEP TO HER BED THIS MORNING.

EVERYONE BEGAN TO DISCUSS FOUQUET. SO LIKE THE KING'S WERE PHILIPPE'S AIR, VOICE AND MANNER THAT NO ONE HAD THE LEAST SUSPICION.

IT IS CLEAR THAT MONSIEUR FOUQUET IS RUINING THE STATE.

MOTHER, I DO NOT LIKE TO HEAR MONSIEUR FOUQUET SPOKEN ILL OF.

NOR DO I LIKE UNNATURAL CRIMES, AND PLOTS TO KEEP THEM SECRET.

SECRET CRIMES! SIRE, YOU SPEAK CRUELLY TO YOUR MOTHER.

SO AGITATED WAS THE QUEEN AT HEARING THESE WORDS, THAT PHILIPPE HAD PITY ON HER. IN HIS HEART, HE FORGAVE HER FOR HIS YEARS OF SUFFERING.

DEAR MOTHER, I WISH ONLY THAT THERE BE PEACE BETWEEN YOU AND MY FRIENDS.

AS TIME PASSED, PHILIPPE BEGAN TO WONDER ABOUT THE ABSENCE OF ARAMIS.

D'ARTAGNAN, WHERE IS YOUR FRIEND, THE BISHOP OF VANNES? BRING HIM TO ME.

BUT SIRE, HE . . .

AT THAT MOMENT, A LOUD VOICE WAS HEARD.

IT IS THE VOICE OF MONSIEUR FOUQUET!

THE DOOR OPENED. THEN PHILIPPE SAW WHAT HE LITTLE THOUGHT TO SEE.

BY CHANCE, LOUIS HAD DRESSED HIMSELF IN THE SAME COSTUME THAT PHILIPPE WORE. EACH WAS TO THE OTHER AS A FORM REFLECTED IN A GLASS.

THEN LOUIS WENT UP TO THE QUEEN MOTHER.

MY MOTHER, DO YOU NOT ACKNOWLEDGE YOUR KING?

PHILIPPE ALSO STEPPED FORWARD.

MY MOTHER, DO YOU NOT ACKNOWLEDGE YOUR SON?

AT THIS, LOUIS TURNED TO D'ARTAGNAN.

LOOK US IN THE FACE AND SEE WHO IS KING. SAY WHICH OF US IS PALER, HE OR I!

D'ARTAGNAN WALKED DIRECTLY TO PHILIPPE.

MONSEIGNEUR, YOU ARE MY PRISONER.

THE KING, REPROACHED BY THE SILENT GAZE OF HIS LONG-TORTURED BROTHER, HURRIED FROM THE ROOM. THEN . . .

IF I WERE NOT YOUR SON, I SHOULD CURSE YOU, MY MOTHER, FOR HAVING RENDERED ME SO UNHAPPY.

COME, MONSEIGNEUR. I AM BUT A SOLDIER, AND MY DUTY IS TO THE KING.

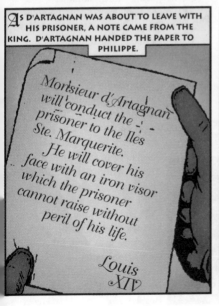

AS D'ARTAGNAN WAS ABOUT TO LEAVE WITH HIS PRISONER, A NOTE CAME FROM THE KING. D'ARTAGNAN HANDED THE PAPER TO PHILIPPE.

Monsieur d'Artagnan will conduct the prisoner to the Iles Ste. Marguerite. He will cover his face with an iron visor which the prisoner cannot raise without peril of his life.

Louis XIV

IT IS JUST. COME, I AM READY.

ARAMIS WAS RIGHT. THIS ONE IS AS MUCH A KING AS THE OTHER.

THE END

THE MAN IN THE IRON MASK
ALEXANDRE DUMAS

"All for one and one for all!"

Even people who have never read *The Three Musketeers* know this rallying cry. With *The Man in the Iron Mask* (of which the Classic Illustrated edition adapts one section), Alexandre Dumas revisits the dashing soldier d'Artagnan and other popular characters from his earlier novel. Like *The Three Musketeers*, *The Man in the Iron Mask* pits its heroes against almost over-whelming obstacles, and lets them romp through adventure after adventure on the way to overcoming their foes. This time, however, they are also pitted against each other, as the gallant d'Artagnan finds himself opposed to the schemes of his old friend Aramis. And because this book is set thirty-five years after *The Three Musketeers*, our heroes are no longer vigorous youngsters at the opening of their lives, but mature men of experience whose best days are mostly behind them. It ends with the deaths of three of the original four heroes. Love, honor, loyalty are still the principal motivaters, but here we see their dark side as well as their promise. Honor must face deceit. Loyalty strives with betrayal. A noble ambition must be sacrificed to a selfish one. Good men are brought low, as scoundrels triumph.

Or do they? For all its moments of sadness, *The Man in the Iron Mask* is a profoundly cheerful book, as full of charm and optimism

as *The Three Musketeers*. We gallop through one escapade after another at breakneck speed, only pausing here for a moment of pure comedy, there for one of deepest melodrama. Dumas could hardly write it otherwise. He was him-self a bubbling optimist. If his heroes and villains were all drawn larger than life, they only reflect their creator him-self, a man who devoured life in all its fullness. He never holds back from sen-timent, even tragedy, but is incapable of gloom.

The Author

Alexandre Dumas (1802-1870) lived a life as flamboyant as his novels. His grandfather was a French nobleman, his grandmoth-er a black slave in Haiti, and his father, the physical model for the giant Porthos, was a general in the armies of the French Revolution who died penniless in 1806 after quarreling with Napoleon. Dumas grew up in poverty, but after he moved to Paris in 1822 he got a good job, read every book he could get his hands on, and turned his hand to writing. He first made his mark in the theater with a string of popular hits between 1829 and 1843, mostly histori-cal melodramas. He began to write novels as well, for news-paper serialization, and his his-torical fiction was even more successful than his plays. Besides *The Three Musketeers* and its sequels, many of his novels are still well-known today, including *The Count of Monte Cristo* (1844-5), *Queen Margot* (1845) and its sequels *The Lady of Monsoreau* (1846) and *The Forty-Five* (1848), and *The Queen's Necklace* (1848-50). He wrote prolifically in other genres as well, including travel books, animal tales, children's stories, and a *Grand Dictionary of Cooking* (1873). He infused his love of action and his delight in the picturesque into all his writing. His output was prodigious: he once claimed to have published 1200 books, and the complete French edition of his works actually comes to over 300 volumes.

And he *needed* to write fast, because as quickly as he earned a fortune, he could spend it even quicker. Dumas's lifestyle was extravagant. A man of enormous gusto and appetites, he built himself a mansion, had dozens of mistresses, gave wonderful entertainments for his large number of friends, bragged and told stories and loved to participate in adventures as well as to write about them. By 1850 he was so deep in debt he had to leave France to avoid his creditors, and he spent years traveling and writing abroad.

The Plot

In *The Three Musketeers* (1844), readers first met the young soldier d'Artagnan and his three friends Athos, Porthos, and Aramis, and followed their adventures foiling the wicked plots of Cardinal Richelieu and the evil Milady. The public loved these heroes, and Dumas returned to them in *Twenty Years After* (1845). We find their careers have taken diverging courses—d'Artagnan is still

in the Musketeers, Aramis has become a priest, Athos and Porthos are simple gentlemen in retirement—but with both France and England in a state of civil war their services are once again needed, and after working for a while at cross-purposes they reunite at last in a good cause. Another ten years have passed before the opening of the final sequel, *The Vicomte de Bragelonne* (1848-50), a very long novel normally published in three volumes, of which *The Man in the Iron Mask* is the last.

When *The Vicomte de Bragelonne* begins we discover that, in spite of all his valiant service, d'Artagnan's career has stagnated; but soon, Louis XIV rewards him with a well-deserved promotion to Captain of the Musketeers. He has lost nothing of his adventurous enthusiasm and cleverness, and the first part of the novel finds him largely involved in engineering the return to the throne of England of the exiled king Charles II. Aramis too has advanced in his chosen profession. He is now Bishop of Vannes, thanks to the finance minister Nicolas Fouquet, and also a rising star among the secretive Jesuits, whose leader he becomes in the course of the novel. Porthos, now a wealthy widower, yearns to cut a figure at the royal court. With his friends'

help he is not only privileged to dine with Louis XIV, but greatly impresses the king with his huge appetite and cheerful naiveté. Aramis also calls upon Porthos's military skills to design and construct fortifications for Fouquet's island of Belle-Isle-en-Mer. The fourth Musketeer, Athos, meanwhile lives mostly in seclusion on his estates. He has devoted many years to the care and education of his only son Raoul, the Vicomte de Bragelonne, who was first introduced as a child in *Twenty Years After* and is much loved by his father's three friends. Raoul has now grown to young adulthood, and is eager to make his own mark in the world. Much of the novel, therefore, follows his adventures at the court of Louis XIV.

Louis has been a king since the age of five, but only now in his early twenties is he beginning to assert his independence from his mother, from his guardians, from the ministers and ambitious courtiers who want to guide and control him. He has learned the danger of depending too much on a single minister, as his father had depended on Richelieu, and distrusts the ambitions of Fouquet, who apparently hopes to dominate his new government. He is vigorous, ambitious, full of plans for himself and for France. But he has not yet learned to walk the delicate line between the just exercise of royal power and its abuse.

Nor has Louis learned how to balance his role as king against his needs and desires as a man. He covets his younger brother's beautiful wife Henriette, and Henriette responds willingly to his flirtation. Her husband is jealous, though, so Henriette and Louis

have to conceal their liaison: they plan for Louis to pretend to court one of the young girls in her entourage. Just to be safe, Henriette selects as their cover a girl with a limp and little money, Louise de la Vallière, who happens to be Raoul's childhood sweetheart and fiancée. The King thinks so poorly of Louise that he refused Raoul permission to marry her—he says Raoul can do much better than that. When the King is thrown into her company, however, he discovers the girl he despised is a beautiful, charming, delightful woman. He falls head over heels in love with her. And Louise, forgetting Raoul, falls in love with the King. Raoul, sent to London to keep him out of the way, knows nothing about this until the jealous Henriette summons him home and reveals the dreadful truth.

Heartbroken by the betrayal, Raoul flees the court. Athos goes straight to confront Louis about his misconduct, proclaiming in righteous anger that a king who abuses his position for selfish ends is unworthy of a gentleman's service. Louis, unaccustomed to open insult and disrespect from a subject, furiously orders d'Artagnan to arrest the culprit and take him to the Bastille.

D'Artagnan has no choice but to obey. But he knows the King's noble impulses as well as his selfish and arrogant ones, and talks him out of his resentment. But after this incident Athos's faith in royalty has been broken, and he returns with his son to their country home in sorrow and bitterness. Months later Raoul, still despondent, joins a military expedition to Africa. Although Athos knows he is seeking an honorable death, he can't persuade his son to stay at home any longer.

At the Bastille with Athos, d'Artagnan had encountered Aramis having supper with the prison governor. D'Artagnan's sudden appearance seems to disturb Aramis, and that starts d'Artagnan wondering, what could his scheming friend be up to this time? (See panel on previous page). Try as he might, d'Artagnan can't figure it out. The answer, of course, is that Aramis is already preparing his scheme to substitute the imprisoned prince Philippe for the real king. Aramis had stumbled on the secret of the royal twins by accident, but at once recognized the opportunity it implied: if he made the king a prisoner, and a prisoner king, the man he had raised out of misery would owe him an enormous debt, which Aramis intends to collect on. For starters he wants to be a Cardinal and Prime Minister. After that, he wants to be Pope! Only by having a king in his pocket can he hope to achieve that.

AND FOR YOURSELF?

FIRST, I WILL BE MADE A CARDINAL AND PRIME MINISTER OF FRANCE. THEN, SINCE I SHALL HAVE GIVEN YOU THE THRONE OF FRANCE, YOU WILL CONFER ON ME THE THRONE OF ST. PETER.

He is successful at first. But as we know, the plot which began so well quickly unravels. Aramis used his position in Fouquet's confidence to engineer the substitution, and considering that Louis had been on the verge of ordering Fouquet's arrest, he reasonably expects his patron to approve a change which will help them both. But Fouquet is aghast that a treasonous assault could

GO AT ONCE — TO SAVE YOUR LIFE. I GO TO MY SOVEREIGN TO SAVE MY HONOR.

have been committed while Louis was a guest in his home. He rushes immediately to extract the real king from the Bastille, only giving Aramis a short headstart to escape and a promise of safety on Belle-Isle. Aramis realizes that he has ruined Porthos by involving him in his scheme and has to take him away with him; Louis will never believe the good-natured giant was an innocent dupe. He still can't bear to confess the truth, though, and Porthos is pathetically confident the king is about to make him a duke, when in fact he's on the run for his life.

Freed from the Bastille, Louis XIV is out for blood. He utterly refuses any pardon for Aramis and Porthos, and is more determined than ever on the downfall of Fouquet, who knows the truth and witnessed his humiliating imprisonment, so compromising to the royal dignity. The hapless Philippe is condemned to life in solitary confinement, his royal face hidden behind an iron mask, forbidden to communicate with anyone. Summoned back to court after escorting Philippe to a distant prison, d'Artagnan finds Colbert's fortunes on the rise, Fouquet's sinking fast. Colbert has "proof" that Fouquet embezzled royal funds; now he and the King can hardly wait to dispose of him altogether. Fouquet knows his doom is approaching—d'Artagnan, who admires him, even tells him to run away while he can—but he puts off escape till too late. In a desperate race on horseback, Fouquet nearly outruns the pursuing d'Artagnan when the musketeer's horse collapses and dies on the road, but Fouquet generously comes to d'Artagnan's aid, and seals his own fate. He will spend the rest of his life in prison.

D'Artagnan didn't like having to arrest Fouquet, but he obeyed his orders faithfully. The King's next command, however, shakes him to the soul: he is to take a troop of soldiers to Belle-Isle, seize the fortress, and kill its rebellious defenders. That means Aramis and Porthos! Torn between his loyalty to his friends and his duty to Louis, d'Artagnan wracks his brain, always so fertile in the past, to come up with a way to save Aramis and Porthos without betraying his King. And he does come

up with several good stratagems—but all in vain. Colbert has foreseen every move d'Artagnan can think of, and has taken steps to prevent him from succeeding. In the end, d'Artagnan is helpless, removed from his command and dispatched back to the king, while strangers take over the job and carry out the task with ruthless efficiency. Aramis realizes there's no hope without d'Artagnan on the scene and orders the defenders to surrender. Still, a slim chance exists for him and Porthos to escape by means of a boat hidden by fishermen in a cave. In a desperate last

Was There Really a Man in an Iron Mask?

No. There was, however, a mysterious prisoner in a velvet mask, who was officially known as Marchiel or Marchioly and died in the Bastille in 1703. He had been a prisoner for many years under extremely tight security. No one ever talked about him. By the time the secret of his existence leaked out, he and everyone who knew the truth had been dead for many years. Beginning in the 1740's, then, the field was open for wild speculation and romantic embroidery. The idea of a masked prisoner—a victim of royal injustice, perhaps—stirred the popular imagination. Alleged eyewitness accounts, elaborate fantasies, tales of royal scandal, elaboration on elaboration circulated freely, and all seem to have led only further from the truth. Who was the masked prisoner? Everyone had an idea—he was Louis XIV's older brother, his son, his cousin, an Italian secretary, a Turkish prince, a woman... As the stories built on each other, the velvet mask became

fur, then iron. The tale of royal twins used by Dumas first appeared in 1790 and quickly became a favorite. Some even claimed that Napoleon was a descendent of the Man in the Iron Mask, and therefore the legitimate heir to the overthrown monarchy. Other alleged descendants cropped up in later years, one as recently as 1911.

And the truth behind the tale? Historians as well as fiction-writers have combed through the scanty evidence and tried to unmask the prisoner without much luck. Many ingenious theories have arisen, but only a few are at all plausible. The strongest arguments seem to indicate that the man in the velvet mask was called Eustache Dauger. But who was Eustache Dauger? Why was he imprisoned for so long, in such an extraordinary way? Unfortunately we still don't know. We may never find out for certain. Truth, it seems, can be much stranger than fiction.

stand, Porthos single-handedly slaughters over a hundred of the king's men. But in the end he can't save himself. On Aramis's instructions he blows up the cave with a barrel of gunpowder, but before he can escape, his legs fail him, an event he had foreseen, the collapsing stones fall upon him, and despite the efforts of Aramis and the fishermen to save him, the giant is crushed and dies. Grimly, Aramis leaves Porthos in this rocky tomb, and makes his escape to Spain. Meanwhile d'Artagnan, confronting Louis in person, has won his friends' pardon. He hastens to Belle-Isle, but arrives there too late.

Porthos in his will left all his possessions to Raoul, but Raoul never returns to enjoy them. Seeking death in battle, he finally finds it despite the efforts of his friends to save him from his own despair. Athos, reduced by grief more than age to an invalid shadow of himself, has a vision of his son's death, and an intimation of heavenly reunion to come. The servant who had gone with Raoul to Africa returns with the sorrowful news, and Athos, receiving this confirmation, slips away so peacefully that his friends, watching, don't even realize he has died.

The novel concludes with the death of d'Artagnan. A dozen years have passed. Louis XIV has begun to achieve the goals of grandeur for himself and for France which he and Colbert revealed at the time of Fouquet's fall. And d'Artagnan still stands beside him, still commander of the Musketeers, still trusted and honored, but increasingly aware that it doesn't means as much as it did in the time of his youth. All glory now is but a reflection of the King's, and d'Artagnan regrets his lost independence. Without his old friends, he spends his days alone in the crowd at court. Even Aramis's unexpected reap-

pearance as an ambassador from Spain is but ironic punctuation. But d'Artagnan still has ambition: he wants to be a Marshal of France, one of the tiny elite of high military commanders. France is now at war with the Dutch, and Louis is able to satisfy this loyal soldier's wish. D'Artagnan is given an army to command, which he does with notable success. His reward is dispatched—official promotion, and the precious wooden baton which symbolizes it. But, in a final irony, the courier arrives almost too late. In the midst of victorious battle, d'Artagnan is fatally wounded. He has only enough time to grasp the Marshal's baton in his hand before dying. It is a moment of glory, and he goes to rejoin his old friends in heaven.

D'Artagnan

The clever, impulsive, warm-hearted youth introduced in *The Three Musketeers* has matured into a resourceful, experienced, responsible officer, well worthy of a king's trust. Less impetuous than he used to be, d'Artagnan is above all a man of ingenuity. There are few problems he can't solve. He can decipher the plotting of others as well; when he repeatedly encounters Aramis in unexpected places, he knows his old friend is up to something, and it annoys him tremendously that he can't figure out what. Clear-eyed, he sees the faults and weaknesses of those around him as well as their virtues; and he makes a clear distinction between

MY BROTHER WILL DISAPPEAR SO SIMPLY ? A SECRET CONTRIVANCE WHICH YIELDS TO THE PRESSURE OF A FINGER WILL LOWER THE BED TO AN UNDERGROUND PASSAGEWAY. IT WILL RETURN EMPTY.

The Characters

virtue and vice, honor and villainy. More than once he is able to persuade Louis XIV, still youthfully impetuous, to reconsider hasty royal decisions and moderate regrettable impulses.

D'Artagnan thinks more carefully now of the consequences of decisions, as well as their expedience. But once he has thought, he quickly translates ideas into action.

D'Artagnan's primary virtue is loyalty. He has served the king with devotion since Louis was a child, and finally comes to find in him a master truly worthy of his service. He is loyal to his friends. Though separated by the events of their lives and the increasing divergence of their personalities and goals, Athos, Porthos and Aramis are as dear to him now as they were as young men in the Musketeers, while Raoul is almost the son he never had. Repeatedly d'Artagnan finds his loyalties in conflict. He has to arrest Athos when ordered, but he lets the governor of the Bastille think that Athos is a dinner-guest, rather than a prisoner, and persuades Louis how unjust the order had been, so his deception becomes reality, and the demands of duty and friendship alike are satisfied. D'Artagnan also has a lively respect for the doomed Fouquet and he treads a delicate line by repeatedly warning him of the King's plans against him, even urging him to flee Nantes before Louis arrives. After the arrest he tells the King frankly he would let Fouquet escape if he were entrusted to his keeping. But once given a direct order to take Fouquet into custody, d'Artagnan exerts himself to the utmost to obey, and Fouquet can only regret having passed up earlier chances to make d'Artagnan a true friend.

While in conflicts of loyalty, d'Artagnan's heart at least hears the calls of friendship louder than any oth-

The Real d'Artagnan

Dumas derived the inspiration for his hero, and various of his associates and exploits, from the *Memoirs of Monsieur d'Artagnan* (1700), a work of fiction by the prolific Gatien de Courtilz de Sandras. Courtilz in turn based his fiction very loosely on the life of a real man. Charles de Batz-Castelmore was born in southwest France around 1615, part of a large noble family which included at least four brothers and three sisters. Along with two of his brothers he used the name d'Artagnan, which properly belonged to his mother's wealthy relatives. Like many young nobles he joined the army, entering the royal Guards around 1635, and was admitted to the elite unit of royal Musketeers in 1644. By the time his

COME, MONSEIGNEUR, I AM BUT A SOLDIER, AND MY DUTY IS TO THE KING.

musketeer company was disbanded in 1646 d'Artagnan had already come to the notice of Cardinal Mazarin, then head of the government, who employed him on a number of delicate diplomatic missions over the following years. By 1656 d'Artagnan had risen to be captain of the Guards. When the Musketeers were reinstated in 1658 he was given effective command over them, and was officially promoted to their head in 1667.

The real d'Artagnan was therefore one of the prominent personages of the day. As a confidential agent of Mazarin, and later of the King, he hobnobbed with all the rich and powerful people at the royal court. Louis XIV trusted him with difficult and controversial assignments. He arrested the powerful Fouquet in Nantes in 1661, watched over him during the subsequent trial, and conducted him to his final prison in 1664. A few years later he did the same for one of the King's own friends, who had imprudently tried to marry one of the King's cousins. D'Artagnan continued to receive promotions and honors, and served with distinction in Louis XIV's wars. On June 23, 1673 he was killed at the head of his musketeers in the battle of Maastricht.

As a man of some renown, involved in many of the most colorful events of his day, d'Artagnan was a natural subject for a fictionalized biography—Courtilz's "Memoirs" were roughly the seventeenth-century equivalent of modern TV movies. They were rather less accurate, however. Courtilz, and Dumas after him, embroidered a whole series of colorful adventures for d'Artagnan which he couldn't possibly have accomplished. (At the time of *The Three Musketeers*, for instance, the real d'Artagnan was a young teenager living at home.) In *The Man in the Iron Mask* Dumas does include some incidents from the life of the original, like the arrest of Fouquet, though the details of the action owe everything to the novelist's vivid imagination and nothing to the rather dry facts of the case. Dumas has also left out the inconvenient fact that the real d'Artagnan married (in 1659), had two sons, and divorced his wife in 1665. Honor and friendship, not family values, are the touchstones of the hero's life in these novels.

ers, his devotion to the king is unquestionable. Faced with both Louis and his twin Philippe after the switch, he never doubts which is which: Louis is the king he serves, Philippe is an impostor, and that's all there is to it. But while he has no sympathy for Aramis's conspiracy, he hopes desperately that

Louis will send someone else to capture the fleeing Aramis and Porthos, because he knows their rebellion must mean their death and he doesn't want their blood on his hands. Knowing his reluctance, the king sends him anyway, as a test, and d'Artagnan fails it by seeking any stratagem he can devise short of direct disobedience to ensure his friends' escape. But Colbert is as wily as he, and foresees every move he attempts. Returning in fury to the king, d'Artagnan reproaches him for his dishonorable commission—a man should not be sent deliberately to kill his friends, or expected to stand by while others do so. Louis acknowledges the point. He will not accept d'Artagnan's resignation; and he will not abuse d'Artagnan's loyalty again.

Aramis

Once a dashing, romantic young man with a taste for gallant intrigue, he chose a life in the Church instead of a career as a soldier, but has never entirely given up the habits of his adventurous youth. Over the years, though, his character has darkened. He loves secrets and conspiracy for their own sake. He has even become (secretly) the head of the Jesuits, whom Dumas portrays as a sinister force with secret agents everywhere. Aramis is ruthless in pursuing his own ambitions and uses other people as tools to that end, his friends as much as strangers (though he does hope Porthos and Fouquet will share some benefits of success in his plot against the King, and sincerely regrets ruining the innocent Porthos when it collapses). Although he talks to Philippe persuasively about righting old injustices, his actual reasons for the conspiracy are selfish: he wants to be Prime Minister and Pope, and to do that he needs a king as ally. He will sacrifice anyone he has to in order to succeed, he will lie to Porthos, deceive d'Artagnan, lay violent hands on the sacred person of the real king, violate every principle of hospitality, and commit whatever fraud, forgery, or falsehood he may require. Aramis is not wholly evil —friendship still lives in his heart, and the only tears he ever sheds in his life are for the death of Porthos. But he is not an honorable man. He is shocked and bewildered by Fouquet's revulsion when he reveals the truth—how could any rational man prefer a king who calls him enemy and has sworn his downfall to one who is ready to be a friend and protector? Because he can't comprehend such a reaction, he made no plans to deal with

it, and that's what brings the whole scheme to ruins. In terms of worldly fortune Aramis is as resilient as a rubber ball—he is last seen as a Spanish duke, an ambassador at Louis's court, an honored guest at the King's own table! But Dumas is explicit in his condemnation of this sinister schemer. We see Athos at the gates of Heaven with his son, and we know Porthos and d'Artagnan will meet him there. But Aramis is destined for somewhere much hotter in the end.

Porthos

A giant in body and spirit, honest and open and touchingly innocent of the darker side of human nature, he has changed little since retiring from the Musketeers, except to grow even larger in girth. Unlike his friends, Porthos married, and through his wife became wealthy. His dreams are of simple pleasures—good hunting, food, good fellowship, the respect and admiration of others. He loves his friends without reserve. He trusts them without question, which makes him a natural dupe in Aramis's scheme. Having too much affection and honesty to deceive anyone, he can't understand duplicity in others. Even when he realizes the full significance of what Aramis has done, he feels sorrow for his friend rather than anger, and stays loyal to him even though he foresees his own death. Porthos is often a figure of comic relief, here as in the earlier books. D'Artagnan finds him in despair on the eve of their departure for Vaux, surrounded by magnificent clothes that don't fit: Porthos feels it demeaning to be handled by tailors, so he has been employing his servant Mousqueton as a stand-in—but Mousqueton had neglected to inform anyone he'd grown fatter than his master! It takes all the ingenuity of d'Artagnan and the comic playwright Molière to provide the giant with a suitable wardrobe for the King's party.

Porthos's foibles are as large as he is. But for all his vanity and gullibility, Porthos is a generous and affectionate spirit, whom no one can know without loving: his virtues, too, are greater than other men's. He dies defending a friend he knows took advantage of him—tragic, heroic, a little over-the-top just as the rest of his life had been. When Dumas wrote Porthos's final scene, the writer's son found him sobbing at his desk. It's easy to understand why. He's not the most intelligent character in the cast, but he's easily the most lovable.

Louis XIV

Some of the characters in *The Man in the Iron Mask* are important figures in history, and Louis XIV (1638-1715) is one of them. His parents had already been married twenty years without children when he was born, so Louis was hailed as a miracle child, God's gift to France; he became king at the age of five. Civil war marked his early reign (as Dumas showed earlier in *Twenty Years After*), and he did not take charge of his own government until his tutor, Cardinal Mazarin, died in 1661. At the opening of this novel Louis is a young man on the verge of independence, well-schooled but inexperienced in the business of kingship, who has spent his life surrounded by courtiers eager to indulge his whims, and by ambitious men anxious to win his favor and take Mazarin's place at the head of his government. Willful and arrogant, Louis conducts his flirtations and love affairs without regard for who will pay the price for his pleasure. He neglects his wife for his more brilliant sister-in-law Henriette, abandons Henriette for Raoul's beloved Louise, and drops Louise in turn for a more spirited

young woman as the novel closes. As a King, Louis doesn't have to worry about the battered feelings of those he injures, or so he imagines, though woe betide those like Athos who offend *him*. Louis's behavior is that of a spoiled child—a very powerful child.

His hatred of Fouquet also has something of a child's jealousy in it, resentment of another man's success and popularity, a juvenile suspicion that the older and more sophisticated man might be secretly mocking him and taking advantage of his inexperience. That makes him all the more eager to support Colbert's relentless persecution of Fouquet, and finally to imprison him for life in a remote fortress. Aramis assumes in his plot that Louis won't be able to endure the helplessness of prison and will die soon of despair in the Bastille. The depth of degradation he reaches in one night as a prisoner seems to bear this out: like Humpty Dumpty, he wasn't made for falling. And at that point in the story, when we have seen Louis repeatedly trample roughshod over good people and abuse his power for selfish ends, it's hard not to feel that he has been a Wicked King who deserves to suffer, and that the innocent Philippe, who has already suffered so much, might not be a better ruler after all.

But Dumas doesn't keep us in suspense for long. The substitution barely lasts a morning. No one, seeing both brothers, has any doubt which one is which. The aftermath reveals that Louis has indeed learned a thing or two about kingship, from d'Artagnan and from his other experiences. Beneath the frivolous playboy exterior lurks a steely royal will, which now begins to show itself more openly. His judgment of other men is penetrating. Louis knows exactly how to appeal to d'Artagnan's pride, for instance, and attaches the loyal soldier ever more firmly to his service despite the personal cost. He has given Colbert his confidence, not because he wants a villainous henchman, but because he sees in him a worthy collaborator who shares his vision of the greatness they can bring to France and its monarchy, which Fouquet in his antiquated principles and inefficiency would obstruct. Louis, unlike his father in *The Three Musketeers*, intends that his ministers should serve him, not vice versa. As King he stands above everyone else, and he will stand alone. No power which does not derive from the King's can be permitted to exist. It is to impress this lesson on d'Artagnan, who still cherishes an old-fashioned longing for autonomy, that he sends the gallant Musketeer to Belle-Isle. And although d'Artagnan, angered and humiliated at being so used, tells Louis roundly that's not an honorable way to treat a gentleman and a subject, he accepts the lesson nonetheless. And Louis for his part has learned generosity. He grants d'Artagnan his friends' lives, though it's too late by then for Porthos, and ultimately even receives Aramis back at court. The proud, selfish boy who courted his brother's wife and stole his subject's fiancée has become a great king, who recognizes greatness in those who serve him.

Philippe

Just as Louis's birth was hailed as a sign of divine favor, Philippe's was potentially a curse. His very existence threatened France with endless civil war, so he was hidden away, and imprisoned in the Bastille when he came too close to learning the truth about himself. He is accustomed to confinement, solitude, helplessness; it has made him patient, but also bitter and cynical. When Aramis comes to him with truths and promises, he's eager to hear more. He gladly agrees to change places with the brother he blames for his misery (unfairly, since Louis knew nothing about him), even knowing the switch would be fatal to his brother. His blood is as royal as Louis's, his intellect as keen, his character marked by suffering rather than self-indulgence. Might he not in fact turn out to be a better ruler, as Aramis suggests?

Dumas hedges on this point. Natural sympathy inclines us to take the prisoner's side. We are assured of his innate nobility, the justice of his complaint, the brutal unfairness of his life-long imprisonment for no other crime than his birth. But his complicity in the plot renders him a criminal at the moment it makes Louis the innocent, bewildered victim. By his actions he has demonstrated a treasonable intent. For such a prince, the king's own twin, what other fate can there be but perpetual concealment and imprisonment? Philippe is less guilty than Aramis, who tempted him, but we can't hold him guiltless. He is a tragic figure, who seldom had any choices in his life, and every time chose wrong.

He is also a purely imaginary character. Louis XIV did not, in real life, have a twin, imprisoned or otherwise.

Fouquet

Nicolas Fouquet (1615-1680) belonged to a prominent family in Paris and made his career in royal administration and finance, becoming finance minister (Superintendent of Finances) in 1653. Money tended to stick to the hands of financiers like Fouquet, and he acquired a considerable fortune by means that were not necessarily corrupt by the standards of the day, but certainly came very close. After Mazarin's death he hoped to succeed him as Prime Minister, but he miscalculated: Louis XIV meant to govern personally now that his old tutor was dead, and he would not tolerate any potential threat to his authority. Fouquet's lavish lifestyle, particularly his magnificent new chateau at Vaux which was much finer than anything the King had, aroused suspicion as well that Fouquet had been embezzling royal funds. In the trial which followed his September 1661 arrest the evidence largely cleared him of the most serious charges, but not entirely. He was sentenced to banishment anyway, and Louis, exercising his royal power of pardon in reverse, changed the sentence to life imprisonment. The brilliant team of designers who built and decorated Vaux went to work for Louis in Paris and Versailles.

COLBERT, MY MINISTER, IS UGLY AND DARK-BROWED. HE IS THE MORTAL ENEMY OF MONSIEUR FOUQUET.

As presented by Dumas, the Superintendent of Finances is still ambitious, but also a man to be admired and loved for his virtues, as well as pitied for his faults and his fate: a great man brought down by lesser creatures. We see him as a man of the world, witty and cultured, generous in spirit, free with his money even when he doesn't have any—not unlike Dumas himself, in fact. He loves women, and women adore him. He collects about him artists and poets and the best minds in France, and they repay his patronage with devotion and the fruits of their labor. To be loved by men of genius is a testimony to Fouquet's own greatness of spirit. Living in high style, he owes money everywhere, but no one can quite believe he's on the verge of bankruptcy: appearances support Colbert's accusations of embezzlement. Fouquet's warm heart puts to shame the jealous meanness of his rival and his rival's creatures, but it also makes him vulnerable to their machinations. Warned about them many times, he doesn't believe in his own danger until it's too late. His instinctive horror at the violation of his trust which Aramis committed reveals the honorable selflessness of his heart; though Louis is his known enemy and Philippe a likely friend, Fouquet can't accept the benefits of a crime committed under his own roof against his guest. By going in person to extract Louis from the Bastille he saves both king and honor, but seals his own doom. The final blow comes in Nantes, where Louis, having isolated him from friends and supporters, orders d'Artagnan to arrest him. Even then Fouquet has one last chance to display his selfless generosity, when a desperate race on horseback seems to open the way for his escape: instead of taking the opportunity, he goes to the aid of the fallen d'Artagnan and instead of continuing on to freedom returns with him to the city and prison. It is a sad fate for a noble spirit.

Colbert

So admirable is Fouquet, as Dumas has depicted him, that we can't help taking his side. He is the maligned innocent, hounded by enemies who are in no way his equal. Colbert, on the other hand, is in every way Fouquet's opposite. Cold, ugly, lowborn, mean and cunning, he is painted by Dumas in the most unlikeable and unflattering colors. Where Fouquet it open-handed and careless with money, Colbert keeps precise track of receipts and expenses—admirable in a finance minister, perhaps, but a miser's trait, which the spendthrift Dumas loathed. Fouquet builds a magnificent chateau and pleasure-gardens not even the King can equal; Colbert barely takes note of his surroundings or appearance except as they relate to policy. Fouquet is honest, while Colbert is so devious he can even out-think that master-strategist d'Artagnan. Everything about him seems repulsive and repugnant.

But beneath the loathsome exterior lies a different man, who reveals himself at the end—a man of vision and grandeur, who will build wealth and prosperity for France, increase its territory, expand its power, foster its cultural flowering, make it the envy of all Europe and the model for all other countries to imitate. So vast are his goals that he can only achieve them with the King's full trust and authority behind him, and no rivals penning him into a narrower field. Colbert has personal ambition, true, and his hatred of Fouquet owes much to their incompatible personalities and habits, but his private objectives are only a part of his larger goal. Reluctantly, d'Artagnan eventually learns respect for him, even admiration. Despite his personal shortcomings, Colbert is the man who will shape the Future, for good or ill, according to his own vision. In principle Dumas obviously prefers the magnificence and generosity of a Fouquet, but he shows clearly that only a man as practical and politically adroit as Colbert could encompass the sweeping transformations he ushered in.

The historical original, Jean-Baptiste Colbert (1619-1683), had been Mazarin's close associate in the 1650s, and in 1661 entered the king's highest Council, where he served as Louis's most trusted minister until his death. He is closely associated with the sweeping administrative reforms which marked royal government in the 1660's, with attempts to encourage French trade and economic diversification through overseas commerce and colonization and the establishment of new manufactures within the kingdom, and with the development of an effective French navy. Far from the scheming, repulsive figure Dumas presents in the novel, Colbert was an idealistic workaholic, who was dedicated to the king's service as well as to the advancement of his own family interests: his brother became Foreign Minister, his son worked at his side and succeeded him in office, and his two daughters married dukes.

Themes

The Man in the Iron Mask is a rousing adventure, a swashbuckler in which events hurtle past the reader in breathless succession. Dumas was writing popular fiction for a ravenous public which devoured his novels as fast as he could churn them out. He painted his scenes and characters in high relief—black and white, noble and villainous, virtuous and wickedness—with little concern for subtlety in the broad strokes of his brush. These sharp contrasts emphasize both the emotional rollercoaster and the moral values which underlie Dumas's imaginative fiction.

The characters of *The Man in the Iron Mask*, for instance, fall naturally into contrasting pairs. Most obvious are the twins separated at birth, Louis the King and Philippe the prisoner. They appear identical in face, but could not be more different in character and behavior. Louis, for all his faults, is king to the marrow of his bones, bred to govern, and we see him learning the lessons which will make him worthy of the role he was born to. Philippe, for all his natural virtue, is an impostor in his brother's place, and knows it. Fouquet and Colbert are polar opposites, one noble, generous, and honest, the other vile, ambitious, and scheming. One makes himself the King's indispensable partner in government; the other, a superior man, spends his last twenty years in prison.

Among our Musketeers as well we find these contrasts, even more strongly here than in the earlier novels. Aramis, always secretive, has grown sinister, willing to sacrifice a king to his own selfish ambitions. So who do we find him teamed with but the guileless, bluff, affectionate Porthos—a man who has never had a truly selfish thought in his life and continues to love and support his friend even as he dimly senses the darkness within him. D'Artagnan combines a shrewd mind with a love of action and navigates with ease the treacherous waters of the royal court, delighting in his ability to out-think his most wily opponents. Loyal beyond question to his king, he still reserves his own vigorous individuality and is careful of his honor. But Athos, once his mentor,

I WILL GIVE YOU POWER. IF YOU DESIRE IT, I SHALL PLACE YOU UPON THE THRONE OF FRANCE.

spends his days in retirement, too proud to bend with a courtier's suppleness, his mind fixed on God and the moral absolutes which d'Artagnan has learned to question. Athos has always been a man of uncompromising honor and principle, but he can't save his son from unhappiness with either principles or a strong sword, and ultimately Athos's very virtues have left him too brittle to rebound from misfortune, while d'Artagnan, the eternal pragmatist, is still resourceful and resilient to the end.

Along with such contrasts in character and attitude, we find in *The Man in the Iron Mask* a set of moral questions, which we are invited to ponder even as Dumas presents his own answers through the action. The position Aramis puts Philippe in is a difficult one. Were those who condemned the hapless prince to a lifetime of ignorance and prison just because he was half an hour younger than Louis justified in doing so, or is "reason of state" insufficient excuse for their cruelty? And is he, in turn, justified in accepting Aramis's proposal and turning the tables on his more fortunate twin, who had no part in the crime? Is the campaign of persecution Colbert and Louis engage in against Fouquet justified either by the Superintendent's faults or by their own political goals which are incompatible with his remaining in power? When the King forces d'Artagnan to choose between loyalty to friends and loyalty to the king, is there a right course of action for him to take? Are there limits to a King's authority, and if so, who sets them? These problems all boil down to one in essence: can a good result ever come from an evil act? The answer is not necessarily obvious. Dumas condemns Colbert for hounding Fouquet, and the King for hating him, but he also shows that Fouquet's removal is indispensable to the grand projects they have in mind for the future, from which great benefits as well as hardship will result. More often, however, evil carries the seeds of its own punishment. Philippe, weakly yielding to the temptations of Aramis, only exchanges one prison for another much worse. Louise de la Vallière, betraying Raoul for the King, is only perhaps guilty of love, but she still bears the responsibility for Raoul's death; and she knows that, while Raoul would have been faithful to her forever, her King is fickle at heart, and will inevitably abandon her for another. Louis, for his part, expiates many of his offenses in the terrible night he spends in the Bastille, and emerges no less arrogant, but more responsible in his exercise of his power. Aramis, the mastermind of the scheme, still enjoys earthly prosperity when we meet him at the end, but eternal punishment awaits him for his crimes.

The dominant themes of *The Man in the Iron Mask*, however, remain those of honor and friendship. The bonds which the four Musketeers formed in their youth remain strong and potent in their hearts despite the changes in their lives. The love of a friend for a friend is the most precious and glorious thing, Dumas tells us, and even through suffering it can bring joy to life.

Study Questions

• Aramis claims that making Philippe king and putting Louis in prison is justified by the injustice of Philippe's imprisonment. Is he correct? Why or why not?

• Why do Louis and Colbert hate Fouquet? What reasons for despising Fouquet, if any, do Louis and Colbert have in common? How are their reasons different? Why does d'Artagnan object to the order to arrest him at Vaux? Is he right?

• Is Louis being a good king in his treatment of the country's financier, or a bad one?

• Why does Aramis need the aid of his friend Porthos in carrying out his plot? What do you think he told Porthos to get him to help? Why wouldn't he tell him the truth?

• Why does Aramis expect Fouquet to go along with the substitution? Why does Fouquet refuse to do so? What would you have done in Fouquet's spot?

• How does Louis react when he learns the truth about Philippe? Why? Is Philippe's punishment justified? Can you think of a more just solution to this conflict that threatens the solidity of the French nation?

About the Essayist:

Beth Nachison is an Assistant Professor in the History Department at Connecticut State University, where she specializes in the history of early modern France. She holds a B.A. from Dartmouth College and an M.A. and Ph.D. from the University of Iowa.